love outpoured

DEVOTIONS FOR LENT 2026

AUGSBURG FORTRESS

Minneapolis

LOVE OUTPOURED
Devotions for Lent 2026

Copyright © 2025 Augsburg Fortress. All rights reserved. Except for brief quotations in critical articles or reviews, no part of this book may be reproduced in any manner without prior written permission from the publisher. Visit www.augsburgfortress.org/info/permissions or write to Permissions, Augsburg Fortress, Box 1209, Minneapolis, MN 55440.

References to ELW are from *Evangelical Lutheran Worship*, copyright © 2006 Evangelical Lutheran Church in America.

Scripture quotations are from the New Revised Standard Version Updated Edition, copyright © 2021 National Council of the Churches of Christ in the United States of America. Used by permission. All rights reserved worldwide.

ISBN 979-8-8898-3730-5
eISBN 979-8-8898-3732-9

Writers: Troy M. Troftgruben (February 18–24), Laura Holck (February 25–March 3), Yolanda Denson-Byers (March 4–8), Felix Malpica (March 9–14), Paul E. Hoffman (March 15–21), Jennifer Phelps (March 22–28), Stacey Nalean-Carlson (March 29–April 4)

Editor: Laurie J. Hanson
Cover design: Alisha Lofgren
Cover and interior images: All images © Getty Images. Used by permission.
Interior design and typesetting: Eileen Engebretson

The paper used in this publication meets the minimum requirements of American National Standard for Information Sciences—Permanence of Paper for Printed Library Materials, ANSI Z329.48-1984

Printed in China.

26 25   1 2 3 4 5

Welcome

God's love has been poured into our hearts through the Holy Spirit. Romans 5:5

Love Outpoured focuses on portions of the apostle Paul's letter to the Romans. In words that continue to speak to us today, Paul lays out foundational beliefs for a life of faith in Christian community.

The daily devotions for each day, from Ash Wednesday to the Resurrection of Our Lord / Vigil of Easter, begin with evocative images and brief scripture texts. The writers then bring their diverse voices and pastoral wisdom to the texts with quotations to ponder, reflections, and prayers.

May God's love pour out into us and through us to our neighbors, churches, communities, and all creation!

February 18 / Ash Wednesday

Romans 1:1, 7
Paul, a servant of Christ Jesus, called to be an apostle, set apart for the gospel of God, . . .
To all God's beloved in Rome, who are called to be saints: Grace to you and peace from God our Father and the Lord Jesus Christ.

To ponder
The goal of the Christian life is that for more and more seconds of each day what we think and do and say is to God's glory, that every moment is worship of the true God instead of various idolatries of our making or of our culture's.—Marva J. Dawn, *In the Beginning, God*

Starting with God

On Ash Wednesday we often ponder practices to do or habits to give up. Those are fine things. But they may cloud the fact that everything we have and all that we are come from God.

Without God, we would not be alive. Without Christ, we would not know forgiveness and eternal life. Without the Spirit, we would be alone in this world. Apart from God, nothing we know or take for granted would exist. This basic point is a fine start to Lent: All we have and know in life is a gift from God. We are not masters of the universe.

Paul grasps this at the beginning of Romans. It leads him to name God and Jesus five times in two verses. It leads him to derive his and the Romans' identity from God in Christ, who sets them apart, calls them saints, extends them grace and peace, and calls them beloved.

Too often in life we act as if everything depends on us. And we miss the point. This Ash Wednesday, more than identifying things we hope to do (or *not* do), let's acknowledge our dependence on God and embrace Christ's invitation to follow him to the cross.

Prayer

O Christ, we acknowledge our need for God, embrace your call to follow, and invite your Spirit to lead us forward. Amen.

February 19

Romans 1:8-10

I thank my God through Jesus Christ for all of you, because your faith is proclaimed throughout the world. For God, whom I serve with my spirit by announcing the gospel of his Son, is my witness that without ceasing I remember you always in my prayers, asking that by God's will I may somehow at last succeed in coming to you.

To ponder

Prayer makes your heart bigger, until it is capable of containing the gift of God himself.—Mother Teresa of Calcutta, *In My Own Words*

Praying for others

Praying for others is one of the most important acts of Christian faith. It's also one of the most undervalued. For most of us, praying for others is the first form of prayer we experienced, often during childhood ("God bless Mommy"; "Help the people in ____"). As a result, many adults overlook how significant it is.

Recently I was going through a tough season of parenting. And yet I had a noticeable sense of God's presence. After a few months, a friend asked about my family and said: "I've been praying for you and your family for some time." Though I can't prove it, I'm sure her prayers played a very significant role in lifting me up during a challenging time. As James writes, "The prayer of the righteous is powerful and effective" (5:16).

At the start of his letter to believers in Rome, Paul thanks God for them. Although visiting Rome is a focus, Paul's unceasing prayer doesn't just make that goal likelier. In praying for the Romans, Paul stands with them across time and space. In praying, he unites with them in thanksgiving, worship, requesting, and receiving—and blesses them.

When have you been supported by someone else's prayers? How can you support someone else in prayer this season?

Prayer

O God, I pray for ____. Grant them what they need, hold them in your care, and extend to us your mercy through Christ our Lord. Amen.

February 20

Romans 1:11-12

For I long to see you so that I may share with you some spiritual gift so that you may be strengthened—or rather so that we may be mutually encouraged by each other's faith.

To ponder

In Africa there is a concept known as "ubuntu"—the profound sense that we are human only through the humanity of others; if we are to accomplish anything in this life it will in equal measure be due to the work and achievements of others.
—Nelson Mandela, in *Mandela's Way*

Faith is not a solo act

The United States and Canada are two of the most individualistic societies in the world. A drawback to this is that we often approach faith individualistically—as if it's simply about "me and God," without influence from others.

Most Christians, historically and globally, have not seen things this way. In Paul's letter to the Romans, he expresses a hope to visit them and anticipates a reciprocal encouragement when he does: "that we may be mutually encouraged by each other's faith." His words depict his and the Romans' faith as a singular entity: "the faith that is yours and mine" (my translation). Paul never thought of faith as a solo endeavor: It was shared, encouraged, and lived out with others.

When I reflect on the most spiritually rich seasons in my life, I notice they have always been connected to experiences of Christian community: summers at Christian camps, seasons of a close-knit Bible study group, service trips with my church, and periods when I relied heavily on others' support.

Following Jesus is not a lone-ranger activity. We did not come to faith without others, and we do not practice it in isolation from others. Our faith is a gift from God, nurtured by community, and inherently tied to others through our shared connection to Christ.

Prayer

Lord, help me to serve others and to embrace the grace of living out my faith in community. Amen.

February 21

Romans 1:16-17

I am not ashamed of the gospel; it is God's saving power for everyone who believes, for the Jew first and also for the Greek. For in it the righteousness of God is revealed through faith for faith, as it is written, "The one who is righteous will live by faith."

To ponder

All that we have been saying amounts to this: [the righteousness of God] is for Paul God's sovereignty over the world revealing itself eschatologically in Jesus. . . . God's power reaches out for the world, and the world's salvation lies in its being recaptured.—Ernst Käsemann, "The Righteousness of God in Paul"

God's saving power

As human beings, we tend to limit God's saving power. The gospel is an example. Throughout history Christians have boiled it down to a specific aspect (or two) of its significance: forgiveness, eternal life, inclusion, affirmation, unconditional love, empowerment, self-improvement, a renewal, a call to action, or a call to justice, for example. While the gospel yields all these things, equating it simply to one of them is profoundly limiting—as if all that matters is "my personal experience." The gospel of Jesus Christ, in short, is much bigger than the ways we often define it and more expansive than we imagine.

In Romans, Paul identifies the gospel as "God's saving power," in which the "righteousness of God" is revealed. As he explains later, this "right-making" is a divine disruption in a broken world. It makes everything new, whole, just, and complete. It restores all that is broken. Through the gospel of Jesus Christ, God's saving power is extended to all. And that changes everything.

God's saving work in our lives is bigger, deeper, and greater than we have the capacity to appreciate. But we don't need to understand everything about it to trust. In trusting God's saving power made known in Christ, we receive all we need for today—and for eternity.

Prayer

O God, grant us your salvation made known in Christ, and we shall have and know all that we need. Amen.

February 22 / Lent 1

Romans 3:21-22
The righteousness of God has been disclosed and is attested by the Law and the Prophets, the righteousness of God through the faith of Jesus Christ for all who believe.

To ponder
Faith, however, is a divine work in us which changes us and makes us to be born anew of God.—Martin Luther, "Preface to Romans"

Faith in/of Jesus Christ
As a pastor, I have had people tell me they didn't "believe enough" or they felt their faith wasn't "strong enough." I assured them faith can take different forms—and coexist with doubt.

But they seemed to think of faith as something *they did*, and whatever they were doing, it wasn't enough.

Paul has good news for us. In Romans, he says God's right-making power ("the righteousness of God") comes through "the faith of Jesus Christ." The Greek phrase used here is grammatically ambiguous. It may be translated "through faith in Jesus Christ" (NRSV) or "through the faith of Jesus Christ" (NRSVue). The first option emphasizes our trust in Christ; the second option emphasizes the faith or faithfulness exhibited by Christ. Either way, trusting Jesus is assumed ("for all who believe").

Why did Paul allow such ambiguity? He could have been much clearer. He uses the same phrase elsewhere (Romans 3:26; Galatians 2:16, 20; 3:22). Personally, I think Paul intentionally captures both emphases: our faith in Jesus and Jesus' faithfulness to us. After all, faith is neither something we do nor something done without us. It is both a gift and something we live out. So is it our faith in Jesus or his faithfulness to us? Paul answers yes.

Christian faith is not all up to us. It centers on both the faithfulness of Jesus and our trust in him. Our faith stems from the One first faithful to us. Whether we "believe enough" or not, Jesus' faithfulness is enough for us.

Prayer

O Jesus Christ, amid our doubts, help us trust that your faithfulness is enough. Amen.

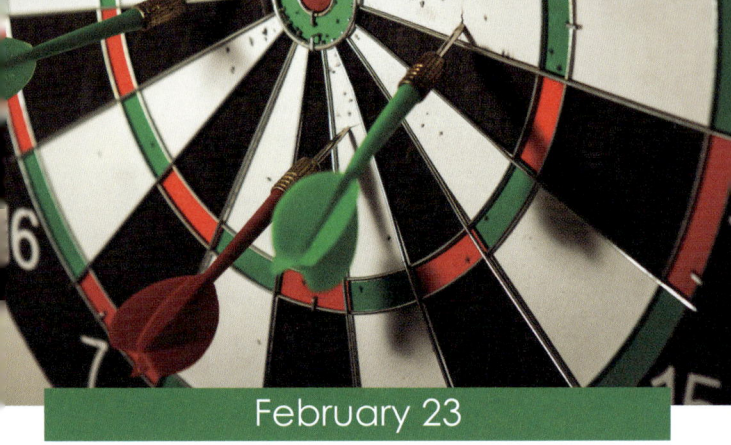

February 23

Romans 3:22-24
For there is no distinction, since all have sinned and fall short of the glory of God; they are now justified by his grace as a gift, through the redemption that is in Christ Jesus.

To ponder
The Christian faith, while wildly misrepresented in so much of American culture, is really about death and resurrection. It's about how God continues to reach into the graves we dig for ourselves and pull us out, giving us new life, in ways both dramatic and small.—Nadia Bolz-Weber, *Pastrix: The Cranky, Beautiful Faith of a Sinner and Saint*

The lost language of sin

Romans makes something very clear: We are broken. Paul attributes this to sin, which is not simply an isolated misstep or mistake. For Paul, sin is an invasive, diabolical power. It's a death-dealing cancer that infects and affects everything we do. Sin is a force we are unable to overcome or escape.

In the wake of past overemphasis on human depravity, the last half-century has seen a pendulum swing toward affirmation: emphasizing our inherent value as God's creation, our belovedness in Christ, and our capacity to do good. While these are true, the gospel is more than simply a word of affirmation. It deals with death and resurrection. If the message "You are enough" were all we needed, we would not need Jesus—and we certainly would not need the cross.

Paul writes that "all have sinned and fall short." Whether we talk about it or not, sin is real. Ignoring it does not make it go away. We are broken and need healing. Something in us needs to die so that we may live. In identifying sin, we welcome Christ's redemption. In acknowledging our incapacity to free ourselves, we embrace grace. As Paul writes later on, "Who will rescue me from this body of death? Thanks be to God through Jesus Christ our Lord!" (Romans 7:24-25).

Prayer

O God, we confess our sin, knowing you are faithful and just and will forgive us, cleanse us, and, through Christ, raise us to life eternal. Amen.

February 24

Romans 4:16
The promise depends on faith, in order that it may rest on grace, so that it may be guaranteed to all [of Abraham's] descendants.

To ponder
Faith is a living, daring confidence in God's grace, so sure and certain that the believer would stake his life on it a thousand times.—Martin Luther, "Preface to Romans"

Faith
In Romans 4, Paul points to Abraham as a leading example of faith. And this wasn't an armchair activity for Abraham: "He grew strong in his faith as he gave glory to God, being fully

convinced that God was able to do what he had promised" (Romans 4:20-21).

Abraham's example shows how faith, for Paul, was more than an intellectual assertion—something like me saying, "I believe walruses are nice." (I have never met a walrus.) For Paul, faith was more than an abstract, theoretical statement. It was a conviction, a trust on which life depends—something more like saying, "I believe this car is reliable," and then driving it on a transcontinental road trip.

The New Testament word for "faith" (Greek, *pistis*) is multifaceted. It may mean faith, trust, confidence, conviction, assurance, belief, pledge, loyalty. We may parse out the nuances, but they all remained for Paul and his hearers as he wrote, "The promise depends on faith." For Paul, Abraham was a quintessential example of faith because he embraced faith in a way that changed the course of his life. Because he trusted God, Abraham packed up everything, moved, planned for descendants, and banked on the impossible being possible.

We sometimes forget that faith is more than an abstract idea. Faith is a total reorientation to a new way of life centered on trusting God. It's what Luther called a "daring confidence in God's grace." This Lenten season, God invites us to embrace faith more fully and authentically—like Abraham did—one step at a time.

Prayer
Lord, I believe. Help my unbelief. Amen.

February 25

Romans 5:1-2
Therefore, since we are justified by faith, we have peace with God through our Lord Jesus Christ, through whom we have obtained access to this grace in which we stand, and we boast in our hope of sharing the glory of God.

To ponder
The world is changed by your example, not by your opinion.
—Paulo Coelho de Souza, Twitter, June 2, 2012

Peace
When I was growing up, "being right" was like an Olympic sport in my family, a kind of intellectual sparring open to any subject, shared experience, or obscure fact. I was not the

oldest, the brightest, or gifted with the best memory in the crowd, and I found myself struggling to find *anything* I could be right about. It was like a string of recurring failed attempts to belong in my own family. All of that trying was futile, of course, because I already belonged and always had. But I didn't experience peace until I was able to reframe the entire context: *Trying to be right about things that don't matter is a complete waste of time.*

Human beings, including you and me, will always experience failure, shame, and separateness when the tool of measurement is opinion and the goal of belonging is either agreement or being right. The fact is, we all have opinions, and we don't always agree. Just like I discovered as a young person, we will never find peace if our highest value is being right.

Peace comes when we give up trying to be right and begin learning what it means to be faithful. Peace comes when we accept ourselves and others as we are, confident that we all belong, even with our disparate opinions. Peace comes when God's grace converts us into people of care and integrity, binding us to one another, teaching us to act from a more grounded center, and flinging us headlong into the arms of God, who reveals mercy after mercy and transforms us into glory after glory, all beyond our imagining.

Prayer

God, interrupt my opinions, justify me by faith, and bring peace. Amen.

February 26

Romans 5:3-5

We also boast in our afflictions, knowing that affliction produces endurance, and endurance produces character, and character produces hope, and hope does not put us to shame, because God's love has been poured into our hearts through the Holy Spirit that has been given to us.

To ponder

Once I had asked God for one or two extra inches in height, but instead he made me as tall as the sky, so high that I could not measure myself.—Malala Yousafzai, *I Am Malala*

Suffering

How can there be a God, when there is so much pain and suffering? "Where is God?" is an obvious question to ask when bad things are happening. But God never promised to shield anyone from difficult things. God promised to be with us.

When difficult things happen, Paul says we can look at affliction as an opportunity to develop our endurance muscles and grow our character. He effectively says that God doesn't send the challenge but instead *pours love into our hearts through the Holy Spirit who is with us.*

Let's look at Malala, a Pakistani girl who, against Taliban law, wanted to learn. When she was fifteen years old, two Taliban soldiers boarded her small school truck, asked "Who is Malala?," and opened fire. Her celebrated recovery and subsequent activism now highlight education rights for girls around the globe. Malala credits God and stands as an example of one who uses whatever happens in life to develop endurance muscles, evolve her own character, and hope in God's love and Holy Spirit.

When you face pain and suffering, ask God to help you develop endurance and character and experience the love that the Holy Spirit has poured into your heart.

Prayer

God, remind me of the love you have poured into my heart. Help me take on my assignment. Amen.

February 27

Romans 5:8, 10
God proves his love for us in that while we still were sinners Christ died for us. . . . For if while we were enemies we were reconciled to God through the death of his Son, much more surely, having been reconciled, will we be saved by his life.

To ponder
You must love in such a way that the person you love feels free.—Thich Nhat Hanh, *True Love: A Practice for Awakening the Heart*

Love

God doesn't withhold love from us. God doesn't wait for us to prove ourselves worthy or good enough. God doesn't wait until we have read the Bible, attended church, confessed, or repented. God doesn't wait at all.

Paul reminds us of this great good news: We don't need to do anything to get God to love us. God's love has been proven to us through the gift of Jesus, God who became one of us and was no stranger to sin, want, or death. He knew friendship and loss, pain and suffering, joy and celebration. Jesus died for his friends and for all of us to prove the power of love over sin and death, that evil might have no hold over us and that we may never be captive to fear. God did all that work while we were not yet born, before any kind of awakening.

Jesus' life was full of healing and joy, friendship and shared meals, walking in nature and talking with people, pondering the meaning of life and of scripture, listening to others, embracing children, and even challenging the authorities that threatened to diminish communal life. He lived without fear and called everyone who followed him to do the same and to teach others this way of life. He meant it for us and for all people for all time.

Prayer

God, where I am bound, free me. Where I am afraid, love and empower me. Amen.

February 28

Romans 5:11
But more than that, we even boast in God through our Lord Jesus Christ, through whom we have now received reconciliation.

To ponder
We might as well tell the truth. And the truth is, the church doesn't offer a cure. It doesn't offer a quick fix. The church offers death and resurrection. The church offers the messy, inconvenient, gut-wrenching, never-ending work of healing and reconciliation.—Rachel Held Evans, *Searching for Sunday*

Reconciliation

Reconciliation implies that a strong, healthy relationship existed in the past. And if we are to believe Rachel Held Evans and Paul, we have been in a messy, inconvenient, gut-wrenching broken relationship with God, and it is our fault.

Today, with Paul, we boast in God. God, it seems, will go to any length to mend what is broken, including taking the blame, paying the penalties, and extending a reconciliatory hand. God is not interested in who is at fault, nor in evening out the cost of reparations. God pays the whole bill, takes all the work, and offers us arms of embrace in return. God wants us in relationship so keenly that God has set up locations across the world to help people come home to reconciliation. We call them churches.

Church at its best throws open the doors to whomever comes, sets a place at the table, and invites everyone to hold out their hands. Into those open hands, the church places bread: the bread of life, the bread of remembrance, the bread of reconciliation. The church holds no authority over the free gifts of God; it is merely a custodian, a mouthpiece, and a place marker for God, who loves all people and is willing to do whatever it takes to restore whatever may be broken.

Prayer

God, bless and hallow your churches, that all people may find your love and grace there. Amen.

March 1 / Lent 2

Romans 6:1-2

What then are we to say? Should we continue in sin in order that grace may increase? By no means! How can we who died to sin go on living in it?

To ponder

We were created to be vessels of God's grace.... A vessel is meant to carry something to someone who is in need, like a glass vial that carries a lifesaving medicine to someone who is ill.—The Most Blessed Tikhon, "Homily for Sunday, August 8, 2021"

Grace

There are at least two ways for grace to abound. The first is to intentionally sin, then seek forgiveness and experience grace. The second is to forget intentional sinning altogether and ask God to make you a vessel of grace. The first is easier, not much change is required, and although you will experience grace, there's not much life on that road. The second is more difficult.

Asking God to make you a vessel of grace is a dangerous idea because God is always looking for such invitations and is not likely to turn you down. It means forgetting the past and opening yourself to a new way of living and being. You will require strength, endurance, character, and a robust prayer life, all of which will be further developed, mainly through trial and error. You will certainly face challenges, even hardships, for who can contain the grace of God? The road before you will therefore be uneven and uncertain, and its end will not be in sight.

But some things will be guaranteed. Boredom will flee and grace will become a place for you—a place you never leave. It will travel with you and companion you. It will reform you and break you and reform you again. You will become a different version of yourself, and you will not be disappointed. All in favor?

Prayer

God, pour out your love and make me a vessel of your grace. Amen.

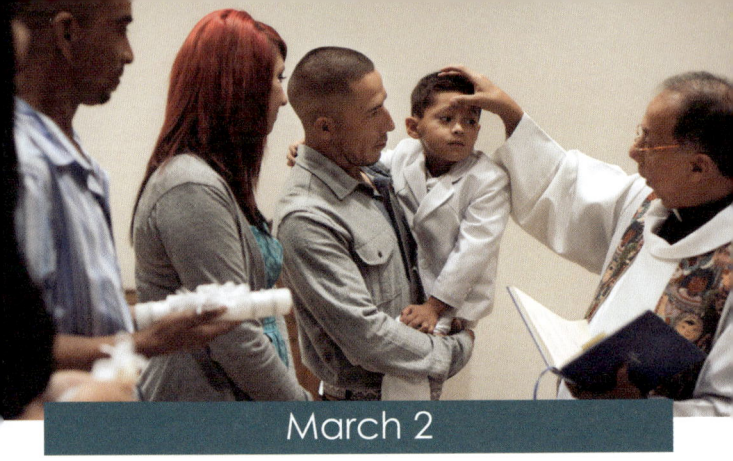

March 2

Romans 6:3-4
Do you not now that all of us who were baptized into Christ Jesus were baptized into his death? Therefore we were buried with him by baptism into death, so that, just as Christ was raised from the dead by the glory of the Father, so we also might walk in newness of life.

To ponder
I have hope because I believe in the God of the resurrection.
—Munther Isaac, *The Other Side of the Wall*

Hope

Hope that is seen is not hope. Hope is belief in something that *cannot* be seen. Munther Isaac writes from the occupied Palestinian territories. For more than seventy-five years, Palestinians have suffered containment, restraint, humiliation, indignity, and oppression. Isaac sees destruction and despair and yet writes about resurrection hope.

Let us have hope too. Warfare, destruction, and discrimination cannot last forever. They take too much effort to sustain, and they are lies. Lies and the forces behind them foist pain and destruction on humanity. We and the rest of the world must do the work of pulling down lies, or we allow suffering and death at their hands.

We were baptized into Christ's death—a death caused by lies. But we are also baptized into Christ's resurrection and into new life. It is a lie that one life is more valuable than another, but someday the truth will be out: We are all beloved of God; we are all valuable; we all deserve autonomy. Resurrected life is our birthright, granted to us from the God of life. And this is the birthright of people everywhere.

Prayer

God of life and hope, empower me with the truth that all people matter. Amen.

March 3

Romans 6:5-8

For if we have been united with him in a death like his, we will certainly be united with him in a resurrection like his. We know that our old self was crucified with him so that the body of sin might be destroyed.... For whoever has died is freed from sin. But if we died with Christ, we believe that we will also live with him.

To ponder

The cross solved our problem by first revealing our real problem, our universal pattern of scapegoating and sacrificing others. The cross exposes forever the scene of our crime.
—Richard Rohr, *Falling Upward*

Sin

Our old selves were crucified with Christ so that *the body of sin* might be destroyed—not the little things we do or don't do, but the one big thing. In the end, the little things we do or don't do are simply symptoms of a larger selfishness that values ourselves and our people above all others. For example, we are relatively fine with war, as long as it's not in our country. We are relatively fine with homelessness, drug abuse, and crime, as long as they are not in our neighborhood or family. We are relatively fine with church closures, as long as it's not our church.

We will maintain our distance and separation from people who are in trouble until and unless we are directly affected. It's just too dangerous, too scary, too much work, too ... something. That's what composes the body of sin: the decision that I am separate from you, that we are separate from them, that the risk of getting involved is too much, and the resulting actions. But in Christ, we die to this idea, our old self, and Jesus sets us free: free to act with love and justice, to work for unity and for human rights—in short, to be one with other people as Jesus is.

Prayer

God, give me courage where I am afraid and give me love to share. Amen.

March 4

Romans 6:9-11

We know that Christ, being raised from the dead, will never die again; death no longer has dominion over him. The death he died, he died to sin once for all, but the life he lives, he lives to God. So you also must consider yourselves dead to sin and alive to God in Christ Jesus.

To ponder

It is no longer I who live, but it is Christ who lives in me. And the life I now live in the flesh I live by the faith of the Son of God, who loved me and gave himself for me.—Galatians 2:20

Alive to God

During Lent, as we draw near to God, who draws near to us, we hear a gracious invitation: Follow me. Jesus invites us to boldly follow him in the way of triumph over sin, death, and the grave. Jesus invites us to fold up our grave clothes and enter into abundance of life.

There is great freedom in knowing that death is never the end of our stories in Christ Jesus. As we follow Jesus, how might we choose to live in the freedom Jesus has afforded us? What does it mean that we are now alive in Christ Jesus—and for what purposes, experiences, and ministries?

As we pray, fast, and give during this Lenten season, God calls us into deeper discernment regarding our own lives and ministries within the kin-dom of God. How can the lives we live be given over more fully to God? After all, to be alive is a tremendous gift, and to be alive *in Christ*, even more so!

Prayer

Dear God, may my gratitude for your abundant life spill over into greater love for you and my neighbors. Amen.

March 5

Romans 6:22-23
Now that you have been freed from sin and enslaved to God, the fruit you have leads to sanctification, and the end is eternal life. For the wages of sin is death, but the free gift of God is eternal life in Christ Jesus our Lord.

To ponder
Oh, freedom, oh, freedom,
oh, freedom over me.
And before I'd be a slave
I'd be buried in my grave
and go home to my Lord and be free.
—African-American spiritual

Oh, freedom!

When I was a child, I was taught that sanctification means "to be set apart for a holy purpose." God's gift to us is the salvation of our souls accomplished by Jesus' finished work on the cross. As we follow Jesus along the winding road to Calvary, let us give thanks for the free gifts of salvation and eternal life.

Now that we are free from earthly masters, scripture teaches that we are enslaved to God. That word *enslaved* is terrifying for those who truly understand the horrors of slavery at the hands of sinful humans. However, when we see ourselves as servants of the Sovereign of love, our fear can dissipate. God has called us for holy purposes. God's own life was sacrificed to secure our own. God, at great cost, paid the price for our sin. God also extends to us the gift of eternal life. We can willingly serve this loving and compassionate God, because this God grants us freedom!

Prayer

God, what would you have me teach others about your free gifts of salvation and eternal life? I want to be obedient to your will. Amen.

March 6

Romans 7:15, 19, 24-25

I do not understand my own actions. . . . For I do not do the good I want, but the evil I do not want is what I do. . . . Wretched person that I am! Who will rescue me from this body of death? Thanks be to God through Jesus Christ our Lord!

To ponder

The saints in being righteous are at the same time sinners; they are righteous because they believe in Christ, . . . but they are sinners because they do not fulfill the law and are not without sinful desires.—Luther, *Commentary on Romans*

Simultaneously saints and sinners

Most humans can relate to Paul's words to the Romans. How I wish I made perfect choices every day. Yet alas, in the words of my teenagers, "I'm just a human, humaning out here!"

Thank God for Jesus, who rescues us from bodies of death. Indeed, scripture teaches that "the wages of sin is death, but the free gift of God is eternal life in Christ Jesus our Lord" (Romans 6:23).

This Lenten season, we are invited to free-fall into the amazing grace of God through Jesus. Although we sin, missing the mark again and again, God's grace is abundant and never runs out!

How might this inform our interactions with other fallible humans? Are we willing to extend the same love and forgiveness to others that we ourselves have received, and want to receive, from almighty God?

How can we look upon humanity with the gentle eyes of Christ? Where have you seen God at work bringing succor to those who are suffering? How can we help?

Prayer

God, alone I cannot solve the problems of the world. Thank you for your church and all who work together to share the life-giving and liberating ministries of Jesus. Amen.

March 7

Romans 8:1-2
There is now no condemnation for those who are in Christ Jesus. For the law of the Spirit of life in Christ Jesus has set you free from the law of sin and of death.

To ponder
Always remember you are braver than you believe, stronger than you seem, and smarter than you think.—Christopher Robin, in A. A. Milne, *Winnie-the-Pooh*

We are not condemned

This Romans passage sounds too good to be true. Could there really be *no condemnation* in Christ Jesus? The world gives us a different message. Daily we are told that we are not good, smart, or attractive enough. Our faults and failures are magnified, whereas our successes and virtues go virtually unnoticed. In fact, there is an epidemic of mental health issues in the United States, as beloved children of God struggle to believe that their very existence matters to anyone, much less to God.

Bless God, for today the apostle Paul reminds us that God does not condemn us. Rather, Jesus' death and resurrection have set us free to experience life—and that more abundantly. All things are possible for God, who "by the power at work within us is able to accomplish abundantly far more than all we can ask or imagine" (Ephesians 3:20). What bold choices can you make because of this? What kind of "stretch goals" do you have hidden in your heart? Would you be willing to risk failure to possibly attain success in Jesus' name?

May we turn to God, free from condemnation, and turn to our neighbors, set free to share the love of Christ.

Prayer

God, help us to see ourselves as you do and to believe that you extend nothing but love and life to us in this world and in the world to come. Amen.

March 8 / Lent 3

Romans 8:3-4

God has done what the law, weakened by the flesh, could not do: by sending his own Son in the likeness of sinful flesh and to deal with sin, he condemned sin in the flesh, so that the just requirement of the law might be fulfilled in us, who walk not according to the flesh but according to the Spirit.

To ponder

Discipline means to prevent everything in your life from being filled up. Discipline means that somewhere you're not occupied, and certainly not preoccupied. In the spiritual life, discipline means to create that space in which something can happen that you hadn't planned or counted on.—Henri J. M. Nouwen, *The Way of the Heart*

A disciplined life

Jesus has put to death the sin that stalks us! In gratitude for this gift, we can make space in our lives for spiritual disciplines that nurture our faith and relationship with God.

The forty-day Lenten journey is a perfect time to start or continue one of the spiritual disciplines that have inspired Christians and the church for millennia. Maybe you can incorporate a discipline like prayer, fasting, or almsgiving into your life. Could you make time for Bible reading, meditation, or a contemplative walk? Is there a labyrinth in your community you could traverse or spiritual music that may feed your soul? How could you embrace a deeper sense of community, love, and solidarity with the neighbors in your life? Think about acquaintances you might invite to your dinner table for conversation, prayer, and deeper relationship.

As many people of faith have discovered, a spiritual discipline isn't another item on our to-do lists. It's a guide for walking "according to the Spirit."

Prayer

God, help me to draw near to you, knowing you have already drawn near to me. Amen.

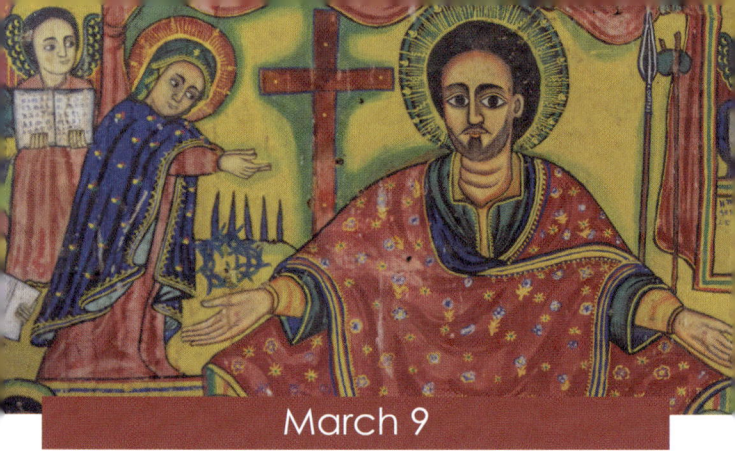

March 9

Romans 8:11
If the Spirit of him who raised Jesus from the dead dwells in you, he who raised Christ Jesus from the dead will give life to your mortal bodies also through his Spirit that dwells in you.

To ponder
As God, the Spirit cannot be reduced to a power source we can tap into (something we can possess and increase in ourselves); rather, the Spirit is the one who encounters us in relationship and empowers us. The Spirit, as God, relates to God's people relationally. The Spirit is not a substance, or a thing, or an effect that we can possess or control. The Spirit is God's own self: the giver of life, our companion and empowerer.
—Cheryl M. Peterson, *The Holy Spirit in the Christian Life*

Your breath, God's breath

The Holy Spirit is in you. The same breath that moved over the waters at creation. The very same Spirit that gave life to Jesus as he brought healing and justice through the hills and valleys of Galilee, Samaria, and Judea. The same breath that lit a fire and created the church on Pentecost. The same breath that empowered modern prophets like the Rev. Dr. Martin Luther King Jr., and the same breath that we share with all living things on this planet.

Give yourself a gift today. Take extra time throughout the day to imagine the connection, power, peace, life, healing, and great potential that is in each of your breaths. You have a direct relationship with God, the one who brought Jesus back from the dead, in each breath. Dwell in this.

Are you feeling your mortality today? Take a breath. Are you feeling low, not sure where to summon the energy for the day? Take a breath. Need to feel connected to something bigger than yourself? Take a breath.

Prayer

God of all creation, let every breath this day be a prayer and reminder that your Spirit is at work giving life, healing, and empowering us. Amen.

March 10

Romans 8:14-17

All who are led by the Spirit of God are children of God. For you did not receive a spirit of slavery to fall back into fear, but you received a spirit of adoption. When we cry, "Abba! Father!" it is that very Spirit bearing witness with our spirit that we are children of God, and if children, then heirs: heirs of God and joint heirs with Christ.

To ponder

As Christians, followers of Jesus, we cannot simply claim that an injustice has nothing to do with us, or that we are too far removed to really understand or to be involved. . . . As Christians, we are called to challenge the structures of injustice, even if we are not directly affected by the injustices themselves.—Munther Isaac, *The Other Side of the Wall*

Cry out

There are many ways for us to cry "Abba! Father!"—through words but also through actions. Each time we treat others as children of God, with love, respect, and dignity, we cry out. When you donate to your local food pantry or volunteer at the local shelter, you cry out. When climate activists work to restore our relationship with creation, they cry out to God.

Last year, I sat in a room of people as an Israeli soldier and a Palestinian freedom fighter advocated for us to come together and work to restore justice in what we have called the Holy Land. They were crying out "Abba! Father!" They were also pleading with us to let our cry be heard.

How might we cry out "Abba! Father!" during this Lenten season? Sometimes the fear is too great and our voices get stuck in our throats. But we have been adopted by God, which means we have no reason to fear. Allow the Spirit of God to come rushing out through you and the church in acts of love, mercy, and justice.

Prayer

God of justice, your children suffer here and around the world. Empower us to cry out your holy name through acts of love, mercy, and justice toward our neigbors near and far. Amen.

March 11

Romans 8:18-21

I consider that the sufferings of this present time are not worth comparing with the glory about to be revealed to us. For the creation waits with eager longing for the revealing of the children of God, . . . in hope that the creation itself will be set free from its enslavement to decay and will obtain the freedom of the glory of the children of God.

To ponder

It is the Windigo way [thinking only of oneself] that tricks us into believing that belongings will fill our hunger, when it is belonging that we crave. On a grander scale, too, we seem to be living in an era of Windigo economics of fabricated demand

and compulsive overconsumption.—Robin Wall Kimmerer, *Braiding Sweetgrass*

Lift up your head

The Indigenous people of Turtle Island recognized that thinking only of oneself would only lead to isolation and death. In the fourth century, Saint Augustine used the term *incurvatus in se*, Latin for "curved in on oneself," to describe the sin of placing the self in the center of the universe. Martin Luther, in the sixteenth century, agreed with Augustine's description. Thinking of ourselves first and foremost distorts our relationships with God, others, and all of creation. We end up using God, others, and creation for our own benefit, instead of developing relationships of reciprocity which enhance life for everyone and everything. When left unchecked, we consume everything around us until there is no life left at all.

Jesus came to lift up our heads and allow us to see God, others, and creation through the lens of God's love, restoring our relationships and undoing the power of sin. Take stock of your relationships. Do you have your own self-interest at the center, or do you place God and others at the center? How might seeing creation as God does affect how you treat it?

Prayer

God of salvation, lift up our heads, release us from the destructive power of sin, and free us to see the world through the lens of your love. Amen.

March 12

Romans 8:22-23

We know that the whole creation has been groaning together as it suffers together the pains of labor, and not only the creation, but we ourselves, who have the first fruits of the Spirit, groan inwardly while we wait for adoption, the redemption of our bodies.

To ponder

All of us need to metabolize the trauma [caused by the myth of race], work through it, and grow up out of it with our bodies, not just our thinking brains. Only in this way will we heal at last, both individually and collectively.—Resmaa Menakem, *My Grandmother's Hands*

Bodies

How often do you pay attention to your body? Have you ever walked into a room and felt that something was off? Did you feel a tightness, a rigidity, a hesitation in your steps? Your body was trying to tell you something, remind you of something, or perhaps was having a trauma response to the environment.

Our bodies carry a lot—more than we know. The internalized traumas of our lives are infused into our bones, muscles, nerves, and organs in ways beyond our understanding. Indigenous, Black, and brown bodies have been scarred by the lie that they are worth less than their white counterparts. Female bodies fear the abuse and judgment so often perpetrated on them. Trans bodies are marked by the sting of prejudice and gatekeeping. Immigrant bodies know the pain of xenophobia and exploitation.

The apostle Paul says our bodies are "groaning"—crying out for healing, for redemption. Our bodies await the new life promised in Christ. As we journey toward Easter and the resurrection, we pray for the healing and redemption of all bodies.

Prayer

God of new life, release us from the bondage of sin and the lies that continue to harm our bodies. Heal and redeem our bodies, that all may experience the freedom and abundance of your reign. Amen.

March 13

Romans 8:26-27

Likewise the Spirit helps us in our weakness, for we do not know how to pray as we ought, but that very Spirit intercedes with groanings too deep for words. And God, who searches hearts, knows what is the mind of the Spirit, because the Spirit intercedes for the saints according to the will of God.

To ponder

Tonight we offer our whole selves as a prayer: Our breathing and our sighing, our singing and our silence. Then we cling to the promise that the Spirit of the living Christ hears those prayers and prays for us, in us, and through us.—Susan Briehl and Tom Witt, *Holden Prayer Around the Cross*

A sigh

Every time I come back to Romans 8:26-27, I remember my grandfather-in-law. He was a man of very few words, especially toward the end of his life. Finally he breathed his last, and I was called on to lead his funeral service. As I met with the family, heard the stories, shared tears and laughter, several questions were raised: Did he know we were there? Did he say "I love you" one last time? Was he able to pray one last time?

The words of Romans 8:26—that the "Spirit intercedes with sighs too deep for words" (NRSV)—came to me loud and clear as a proclamation and a promise. Yes, the Holy Spirit could take even our loved one's sighs, groans, and labored breathing as the most precious of prayers. Yes, he proclaimed his love for his family through a Holy Breath that knew his heart inside and out. He may not have been able to verbalize his last testament, but it was perfectly clear in and through the Spirit of God.

Even when words fail you, know that even a sigh or a groan is enough, beautifully and wonderfully enough.

Prayer

Focus on your breath for as long as you desire. You do not need words. Just release all of yourself into the gracious keeping of God's hands. The Holy Spirit will do the rest. When you are ready, say "Amen."

March 14

Romans 8:28
We know that all things work together for good for those who love God, who are called according to his purpose.

To ponder
There is a thunderous abundance
above us and under us
within us and beyond us
for us and because of us …
that pours from the pores of us
it stores up until it restores us
our source will always resource us.
—Joe Davis, *Unearthing Us*

All for good?

Let's be honest. Do things always work out the way we want them to? No. Is everything that happens in our lives good? No. Does that mean that we do not love God? No. Bad things do happen, even to those who love God.

I do believe God can use anything for good. I would never dare to say that cancer is a good thing—I have loved and lost too many to say that. But I can say that I have known people who have received incredible strength of faith and character after a cancer diagnosis, living life in a way they had not lived before. I also would not call a global pandemic in which millions died a good thing, and yet the pandemic offered an opportunity to break the church open and remind us that we can do hard things, we can change, we can innovate, we can come together, even when it seems impossible.

While not all things are good in the moment, I do know that God has the capacity to make life out of death, wholeness from brokeness, joy from lament. This is good news!

Prayer

God of new beginings, remind us, amid difficult circumstances that tempt us to stray from you, that you are the God of resurrection, bringing life abundant out of the deserts of our lives. Amen.

March 15 / Lent 4

Romans 10:9, 12-13

If you confess with your mouth that Jesus is Lord and believe in your heart that God raised him from the dead, you will be saved. . . . For there is no distinction between Jew and Greek; the same Lord is Lord of all and is generous to all who call on him. For "everyone who calls on the name of the Lord shall be saved."

To ponder

We have to allow what is good, beautiful, and meaningful in the other's tradition to transform us.—Thich Nhat Hanh, *Living Buddha, Living Christ*

Expanding the circle

What an interesting scripture to ponder on a Sunday. Those of us who are "Greeks" should remember that each weekend our Jewish siblings also have a day of Sabbath. In this passage, Paul, a Jew, reminds us that Christ is generous to Jews and Christians alike. He goes on to say that Jesus' generosity extends to all who call on the name of the Lord.

Many of us live in fear of the unfamiliar. Yet here we are encouraged to see among all people a common thread, Jesus' generosity. Jesus' lack of distinction among God's children led him to pray for his enemies, even those who crucified him.

As we open ourselves to those who appear least like us, we are bound to find that we have more similarities than differences. For starters, we are all part of the human family, created by God. In dialog with those outside our usual circles, we find opportunities for our own growth and transformation.

Transformation is the vocation of the baptized people of God. In baptism's waters we were joined to Christ's death, and we emerge from them as children of life. Seeing all people as beloveds of God is transformational thinking. When we are attuned to the possibility of change through encountering those different from us, our lives are expanded and enriched. The world is expanded and enriched as well.

Prayer

God of no distinctions, open our eyes to see you in every person, everywhere. Amen.

March 16

Romans 10:14-15, 17

How are they to call on one in whom they have not believed? And how are they to believe in one of whom they have never heard? And how are they to hear without someone to proclaim him? And how are they to proclaim him unless they are sent? . . . So faith comes from what is heard, and what is heard comes through the word of Christ.

To ponder

The ears are the birth canal of faith.—Mark S. Hanson, installation service, September 15, 2013

God's toolbox

We are very quick to refer to God as creator, but rarely do we speak of what is in the creator's toolbox. Genesis 1 beautifully and systematically tells the story of God's creative work, but the only tool that God uses is the word. God speaks, and each element of the universe comes into being.

In today's text from Romans, Paul writes about the beginnings of faith in a similar way: "Faith comes from what is heard, and what is heard comes through the word of Christ." Through Christ, God again shares a living word, and in us faith comes into being. The moon and sun and stars, even humans themselves, cannot say no to God's creative force. God desires it. God speaks it. It happens.

As is often the case in the biblical story, it's not all about us. God the creator, Christ the redeemer, and the Spirit that sustains us are the actors. Into our open, waiting ears and lives their loving word arrives, and in us faith is born.

Prayer

Creator God, Savior Christ, Holy Spirit, open us each day to the wonder of your word, that faith may be born in us again and again. Amen.

March 17

Romans 11:29
The gifts and the calling of God are irrevocable.

To ponder
I am certain in my heart that all I am I have received from God.—Saint Patrick

Irrevocably gifted
Against all odds, Patrick persevered in his mission to bring the gospel of Jesus to Ireland. After six years as a captive and indentured servant in Ireland, Patrick was able to return to his British homeland. Eventually, he felt called to return to Ireland

as a Christian missionary. Patrick ventured back to enemy territory, armed with the certainty that all he was and the gifts he had were from God.

Where is your "Emerald Isle"? In each of our daily encounters with others, we can share the love of Christ as Patrick did. We are called to bring the good news to those in our day who have not yet heard of love as boundless as that of Jesus. Certain that everything we are comes to us from God and that the gifts God has given us will not be taken from us, we can move into the world in confident faith. As we speak words of love and compassion, offer gifts of kindness and mercy, and work for dignity and equity for all people, the infinite spiral of love continues.

Prayer

O Jesus, keep us steadfast in faith, remembering that your love and mercy can never be taken from us. Amen.

March 18

Romans 11:33, 36
O the depth of the riches and wisdom and knowledge of God! How unsearchable are his judgments and how inscrutable his ways! . . . For from him and through him and to him are all things. To him be the glory forever. Amen.

To ponder
O love, how deep, how broad, how high,
beyond all thought and fantasy,
that God, the Son of God, should take
our mortal form for mortals' sake!
—"O love, how deep," ELW 322

That's a whole lot of praise

Right here in the middle of the week, on an ordinary Wednesday, this text calls for our highest praise. Paul calls us to praise God because God is like no other. All things come from God, and there is depth, wisdom, and knowledge in God alone.

What might Wednesday praise look like, right here in the middle of Lent? It could look much like these devotions, or prayer, or perhaps even midweek worship. But could it also look like offering ourselves to the One deserving of glory forever? Without the inscrutable ways of God to serve as our guide, we can do nothing. At our best, we are instruments of the Holy Spirit, at work in the world, on God's behalf, to let those around us know what God's love is like.

Wednesday praise of the one whose judgments are unsearchable, whose ways are inscrutable, means being our best selves. We cannot do this without the help and grace of the One we are praising. Our union with God makes a complete circle. We are held to hold others. We are loved to love others. We are healed to heal others. The grace of God is a river rather than a pond. Our Lenten, Wednesday, best selves flow from God, through us, to a world in need.

Prayer

Gracious One, it is from you that all things have their beginning. It is also to you that they return. Let my praise flow in your circle of love. Amen.

March 19

Romans 12:1-2

I appeal to you therefore, brothers and sisters, on the basis of God's mercy, to present your bodies as a living sacrifice, holy and acceptable to God, which is your reasonable act of worship. Do not be conformed to this age, but be transformed by the renewing of the mind, so that you may discern what is the will of God—what is good and acceptable and perfect.

To ponder

It was such a pleasure to sink one's hands into the warm earth, to feel at one's fingertips the possibilities of the new season.
—Kate Morton, *The Forgotten Garden*

Getting our hands dirty

Lent, meaning "to lengthen," takes its name from the seasonal change in which we in North America currently find ourselves. The cycle of changing seasons here never grows old. To watch the decay of winter yield rich and abundant soil in which the new season's seeds will grow and flourish is another miracle of God's great design.

God offers each of us an equally miraculous transformation—to move from sinner to redeemed in the waters of holy baptism. Martin Luther taught that this is a *daily* transformation. We are "transformed by the renewing of the mind" with each new day. Every sunrise is a resurrection. Each dawn is Easter day.

Even as this Lenten season invites us to "to sink one's hands into the warm earth," Christ invites us to sink our spirits into the wonderful news of God's new creation. Our eternal life with God has already begun. The world is waiting for us to meet its aching needs and bring the message of renewal and hope to all who need it. The garden is waiting. It's time to get our hands dirty.

Prayer

God of transformative grace, I give thanks this day for the gift of my baptism and the renewal it offers me with each new dawn. Strengthen me to bring your renewal and hope into the world. Amen.

March 20

Romans 12:4-5
As in one body we have many members and not all the members have the same function, so we, who are many, are one body in Christ, and individually we are members one of another.

To ponder
Christianity isn't meant to simply be believed. It's meant to be lived, shared, eaten, spoken, and enacted in the presence of other people. They remind me that, try as I may, I can't be a Christian on my own. I need a community. I need the church.—Rachel Held Evans, *Searching for Sunday*

Be a busybody

One of my mother's repeated warnings when I was a child was "Don't be such a busybody!" You can imagine times when she might have said this. Maybe I was overly interested in an adult conversation, or I wanted to do the things my brother (five years older) was doing. You get the picture.

I didn't realize it at the time, but now it seems to me that the apostle Paul *wants* us to be busybodies, at least in a certain way! Don't get me wrong, I don't think Paul is saying that we should be in everybody else's business. But I *do* think he is encouraging us to know enough about one another, and have enough respect for one another, that we get the work of the gospel done with efficiency and grace.

Without the connection that God plans for us to have with one another, the human community does not function as God intends. Even though we are many, and have different gifts, together we are called to be loving busybodies (or a loving, busy body of Christ) for sharing the gospel!

Prayer

Gracious creator of every living being, help us to be deeply involved and deeply curious about our role in the grand design of all creation. Amen.

March 21

Romans 12:6-8
We have gifts that differ according to the grace given to us: prophecy, in proportion to faith; ministry, in ministering; the teacher, in teaching; the encourager, in encouragement; the giver, in sincerity; the leader, in diligence; the compassionate, in cheerfulness.

To ponder
We need to give each other space so that we may both give and receive such beautiful things as ideas, openness, dignity, joy, healing, and inclusion.—Max De Pree, *Leadership Is an Art*

A mosaic of potential

What if we were all the same? Ugh, how distressing to imagine! If we were all the same, there would be so many limitations on the possibilities of the human family. If there were science without art, melody without harmony, wealth without generosity, and so on, what a limited world this would be.

God's vision from the beginning of creation has been far more expansive. God's grace allows for and encourages broad and inclusive possibilities for who we are and what we can become, together. From the get-go, God intended for us to exist side by side, harmoniously receiving and engaging the contributions that all have to offer.

Our self-centeredness often deprives us of such an expansive vision. This Lenten season of reflection is an opportunity to recenter ourselves in all the possibilities of life in Christian community. We are a mosaic of potential when we give one another space to blossom into the fullness of who God created each of us to be. Like a beautifully harmonized choir, the human community sings beautifully when each person contributes to the whole out of the abundance of gifts with which God has blessed them.

Prayer

Gracious One, thank you for the unique gifts that you have given each of us, your children. Help us to complement our siblings rather than compete with them. Amen.

March 22 / Lent 5

Romans 12:9-13
Let love be genuine; hate what is evil; hold fast to what is good; love one another with mutual affection; outdo one another in showing honor. Do not lag in zeal; be ardent in spirit; serve the Lord. Rejoice in hope; be patient in affliction; persevere in prayer. Contribute to the needs of the saints; pursue hospitality to strangers.

To ponder
I have come to believe that the true mystics of the quotidian are not those who contemplate holiness in isolation, reaching godlike illumination in serene silence, but those who manage

to find God in a life filled with noise, the demands of other people and relentless daily duties that can consume the self.
—Kathleen Norris, *The Quotidian Mysteries*

Godly noise

There is so much to do! The temptation of daily life is to be consumed, to serve the to-do list, and to get lost in the noise. It is no wonder that we sometimes admire the mystics who retreat into silence and isolation, seeking connection to God in the stillness.

Yet Paul's to-do list for the believer in the Christian community is long and fervently pressing. Paul urges us not toward isolation but into community: Be zealous and ardent in serving; rejoice with patience and perseverance. Give, pursue, and love, spurred on by a competitive spirit. Even more, Paul leads us into our daily tasks and relationships with a spirit of generosity and promise. God is in the noise of everyday life.

It is a challenge to find the blessing of the quotidian, the everyday, mundane tasks of life that fill our days. God is not limited to silence and contemplative spaces. God is also abundantly present in the relentless race that we are already running in our daily, busy lives.

Prayer

God of life, inspire us to persevere in your spirit of generosity and hope in our daily lives. Give us glimpses of joy as we love, serve, grieve, pray, and give in the name of Jesus Christ. Amen.

March 23

Romans 12:14-18

Bless those who persecute you; bless and do not curse them. Rejoice with those who rejoice; weep with those who weep. Live in harmony with one another; do not be arrogant, but associate with the lowly; do not claim to be wiser than you are. Do not repay anyone evil for evil, but take thought for what is noble in the sight of all. If it is possible, so far as it depends on you, live peaceably with all.

To ponder

Sometimes, the elevation of harmony over everything else merely makes a gathering dull. Often, though, it is worse than that: The goal of harmony burrows its way into the core of the

gathering and becomes a kind of pretender purpose, hampering the very thing the gathering was supposed to be about.
—Priya Parker, *The Art of Gathering*

The dance of harmony

To live in harmony sounds delightful and calls to mind pleasing arrangements of melodies and delight. When we hold to a definition of harmony as the absence of tension and discord, however, we flatten the range of human experience, freeze the moment, and dull the exquisite diversity of God's creation.

The true nature of harmony in music is a dance between dissonance and resolution. The delight is in the discordant tones and the intriguing juxtapositions of sound that build tension and reach toward resolution. Exquisite harmony savors the contrasts and invites us to lean in and pay attention.

Living in community in Christ calls us to lean into the dissonance of the ups and downs of life and the diversity of God's beloved. We are called to humbly listen and join the dance—especially in the dissonance and discord. For in that tension, we glimpse the purpose and delight of God's presence in every movement of our human experience.

Prayer

God of life, open our hearts to delight in the harmonies of the community of Christ. Draw us into the dissonance and reveal your presence in the dance of life in the fullness of your creation. Amen.

March 24

Romans 12:20-21

"If your enemies are hungry, feed them; if they are thirsty, give them something to drink, for by doing this you will heap burning coals on their heads." Do not be overcome by evil, but overcome evil with good.

To ponder

If we seriously think about it, it probably makes more sense to assume this is a naturally evil world that has somehow been mysteriously "contaminated" by goodness, rather than the other way around. The mystery of goodness is even greater than the mystery of evil.—M. Scott Peck, *People of the Lie*

Contaminated by love

It often feels like we are in a tug-of-war between good and evil. We place our own ways, our own experiences, our own judgments above those of others. We are quick to rail against the one who cut us off in traffic or to vent against wrongdoers. Jesus' command to love one another goes unheeded as we take on righteous anger and quickly make enemies of those who cause us harm. We are familiar with the lust for vengeance that we hope will satisfy. But paradoxically, wounding our enemies only ignites a cycle of retaliation that never ends. Letting go of this cycle feels like defeat, and we fear that evil will contaminate everything for which we hope.

Yet God has the power to end the consuming centrifugal forces of evil that defy God's reign of grace and love. God declared creation good. In Christ, God reveals that love is stronger than evil. And the goodness of love has the power to end the cycles of hate and harm. In the face of our enemies, we are commanded to act with an infectious, counterintuitive care of the other. In so doing, evil cannot and will not prevail.

Prayer

God of love, infuse our lives with the mystery of your goodness so that we are inspired to overcome evil with your loving justice and grace. Use our righteous anger to fuel acts of kindness that reveal the transformative power of your love shown to us in Jesus Christ. Amen.

March 25

Romans 13:9-10
The commandments, "You shall not commit adultery; you shall not murder; you shall not steal; you shall not covet," and any other commandment, are summed up in this word, "You shall love your neighbor as yourself." Love does no wrong to a neighbor; therefore, love is the fulfilling of the law.

To ponder
Don't make the same mistakes that everyone else makes. Make wonderful mistakes. Make the kind of mistakes that make people so shocked that they have no other choice but to be a little impressed.—Jenny Lawson, *Furiously Happy*

Impressive love

I remember hearing, when I was a child, all the "don'ts" loud and clear. "Don't touch that!" "Don't go there!" "Don't say that!" The adults around me tried to keep me safe by cautioning me and pointing out the boundaries around the things that might harm me. It worked—sometimes too well. I came to fear making a mistake.

We often hear criticism and restrictions louder than we hear praise and encouragement. The negatives shout limits at us while the positives whisper inspiration. Both have their usefulness. However, the imaginative possibilities empower so much more than restrictions ever will.

Paul reiterates Jesus' summation of the law, which turns the restrictive "shall nots" into imaginative "shalls." In so doing, Jesus and Paul turn our focus away from the fear of mistakes to the possibility of imaginative inspiration.

In this law of love, God calls us to risk an outrageous abundance of care that the world may deem to be in error. Christ calls us to a generosity to our neighbors that is shockingly impressive. God's love makes no mistakes. When we are filled to overflowing with this love, we need not fear the limits. We can err on the side of extravagant service.

Prayer

God of abundance, your grace reveals extravagant love and generosity. Free us from fear and inspire us to shock the world with impressive love in Jesus Christ. Amen.

March 26

Romans 14:7-9
We do not live to ourselves, and we do not die to ourselves. If we live, we live to the Lord, and if we die, we die to the Lord; so then, whether we live or whether we die, we are the Lord's. For to this end Christ died and lived again, so that he might be Lord of both the dead and the living.

To ponder
When it is hard to know what will happen, it is hard to know what to do. But the challenge, I've come to see, is more fundamental than that. One has to decide whether one's fears or one's hopes are what should matter most.—Atul Gawande, *Being Mortal*

Flourishing hope

We spend a lot of time and energy worrying about the future and what will happen next. Often, anxiety and fear paralyze us, preventing us from taking the next step or risking a choice that may be wrong. If we do nothing, it seems as if we risk nothing. However, our unresponsiveness may reveal a crisis of faith.

Paul reminds us that our lives are completely and wholly in the hands of God. In our life and in our death, we rest in the grace God has already revealed, enacted, and promised. We have nothing to fear—and we have everything for which to hope. Christ is with us in life, in death, in suffering, and in joy.

Time moves on and the future is here, whether we intentionally decide on our next steps or resist decisions because we are overwhelmed with fear. When we listen to the unwavering promise of Christ, we are drawn away from the weight of our fears, so that hope can be revealed as the fundamental foundation of life. When hope matters most, life flourishes and grows into the future.

Prayer

God of hope, release us from the confines of fear and fill us with the hope of your abiding love. Help us to trust in your life-giving grace, so we can step confidently into the future you have prepared for us in Jesus Christ, our Savior. Amen.

March 27

Romans 14:13
Let us therefore no longer pass judgment on one another, but resolve instead never to put a stumbling block or hindrance in the way of a brother or sister.

To ponder
Whenever someone tells their story, you are standing on holy ground. You behave differently, hear them differently, and react from a different place. It's so much harder to hate when someone has shown you their heart.—Michael B. Curry, *Love Is the Way*

Holy connection

As I observe strangers out in the world, I often wonder what their story is. Who are they? Where are they from? What are their struggles? Their joys? Sometimes my curiosity inspires me to strike up a conversation!

Listening to each other's stories is an exercise of shared vulnerability. When I listen to another, I must lay aside my preconceived notions and assumptions to receive their experience. When I share my story, I risk revealing a piece of myself that may be tender or injured. As we expose our experiences, we risk stepping out from behind our protective walls to humbly find glimpses of ourselves in the other person.

While this sounds like a pleasant experience with the ones we love, it is far more challenging with those who come from a different place. If we pause to listen to the stories of our enemies, we risk beginning to feel empathy for them or having the spotlight turned to our own shortcomings.

Our judgments, assumptions, and prejudices can be overcome by connecting to one another through sharing stories and reaching out with the hope of connection. In so doing, we begin to love one another as God loves each one of us.

Prayer

God of all, help us to pause to share stories with one another. Inspire us to reach out and delight in the vulnerability of connecting with people who are different from us, following the example of Christ, our Savior. Amen.

March 28

Romans 14:19
Let us then pursue what makes for peace and for mutual upbuilding.

To ponder
This identification with people so different from ourselves is really wonderful but also extremely difficult, because instead of claiming control in these relationships we open ourselves to an unknown future with many surprises.—Henri J. M. Nouwen, *Home Tonight*

Pursuing surprise
The scenario is familiar to those who watch action movies and thrillers: At some point, there will be a pursuit when someone

or something is chased with exhilarating fervor and thrilling action. We watch with anticipation, awaiting the resolution, when the pursuer and the pursued come together.

Paul invites us into a pursuit of peace and mutuality that is not passive or docile. Rather, we are called to act with fervor and intensity, to enter into the action of God's reign that flows through our world. Can you imagine the coming resolution when God, the pursuer, makes the world whole again?

Entering the pursuit is challenging when we can't fully imagine the resolution. Our imaginations aren't as big as God's and the path to healing and reconciliation is fraught with difficult challenges. There will be twists and turns we don't anticipate, reminding us that we are not directing the action. We will be startled and surprised when God draws us into paths that are beyond our control.

God, however, promises a resolution: peace and mutuality. Christ revealed the hope and power of that promise by rising from the dead for the sake of the whole world. The promise fuels us to join in the action, to enjoy the thrill of the pursuit. We trust that God will draw us into a future filled with imaginative grace that surprises and delights.

Prayer

God of action, fuel us with the power of your promise, so that we may join you in the pursuit of peace and mutuality for the sake of the whole world. Surprise us with grace beyond our imagination through Jesus Christ. Amen.

March 29 / Sunday of the Passion

Romans 15:5-6
May the God of steadfastness and encouragement grant you to live in harmony with one another, in accordance with Christ Jesus, so that together you may with one voice glorify the God and Father of our Lord Jesus Christ.

To ponder
The present age isn't in need of any more Christians. We need followers of Jesus who go where Jesus would go, who try to do what Jesus did, and try to do the greater things that he said we would do.—Neichelle R. Guidry, *Curating a World*

Elusive harmony

I'm a singer who desperately wishes she could harmonize without having the notes in front of her. I admire those singers for whom harmonizing comes unbidden. I'm filled with "holy envy," as my internship supervisor used to say.

It's one thing to sing harmoniously; it's another thing to live harmoniously. There are days when I look at today's world, torn apart by violence and hatred, and I can't even imagine all of us living in harmony with one another. It seems impossible.

Jesus knew something about conflict and discord. He rode into Jerusalem to shouts of "Hosanna!" The crowds rejoiced at the coming of their king. How quickly, though, those songs of praise turned to cries for Jesus to be crucified.

On this day in the church year, when we are made so viscerally aware of humanity's fickleness, let this blessing from Paul's letter to the Romans be the lullaby whispered in your ear. Feel your worry dissipate. Nothing is impossible with God.

Jesus, the crucified king, conducts creation's choir. With his dying breath, he teaches us the song of infinite forgiveness. He silences all those forces that rebel against God, directing our days and our deeds in peace. We may not be able to hear the harmony quite yet, but it's here, because Jesus is here.

Prayer

God of surprising possibilities, we sing your praises! Lead us in the way of Jesus, that we might live in harmony with all creation. Amen.

March 30

Romans 15:13
May the God of hope fill you with all joy and peace in believing, so that you may abound in hope by the power of the Holy Spirit.

To ponder
You do not get to live your life without losing hope altogether now and then. If you haven't ever rocked back on your heels and wondered why you even bothered, then I have to wonder if you even tried.—Sarah Bessey, "It's No Small Thing"

Running on empty
Twice in a six-month period, I ran out of gas while driving. It would be convenient to blame the low-fuel warning light in my

vehicle, but it came on exactly when it was supposed to. The issue was that I dismissed it, thinking I had enough fuel to make it to my destination. I learned the hard way that it's best not to press on fueled only by wishful thinking.

Vehicles aren't powered by wishful thinking; neither are human beings. We need something solid and trustworthy, something truer than anything we can manufacture on our own. We need something we can depend on when things don't turn out as we hoped they would, when we're fearful of the future, when we're overwhelmed by the concerns and complexities of life.

We need God-given hope.

When you are joined to Christ in the waters of baptism, his trust in God's faithfulness is yours. His confidence in God's compassion is yours. His hope for a world made new is abounding in you.

God fills our tanks with the joy and peace of Christ—a peace that surpasses all understanding, a joy that transforms pain—and by the power of the Holy Spirit we are filled to overflowing with that death-defeating hope that fuels lives of love.

Prayer

God of hope, we falter, but you never do. Fill us this day with the joy and peace of Christ, who journeyed through this Holy Week for the sake of the world you so love. Amen.

March 31

Romans 15:15-18

On some points I have written to you rather boldly by way of reminder, because of the grace given me by God to be a minister of Christ Jesus. . . . In Christ Jesus, then, I have reason to boast of my work for God. For I will not be so bold as to speak of anything except what Christ has accomplished through me.

To ponder

Wherever one person takes another into the care of their heart, they have the power to bless.—John O'Donohue, *To Bless the Space Between Us*

It's not about you

When you donate your kidney, you hear things like this: "You're a hero. You're amazing." This was my experience, and the reason I was reluctant to even share my story in the beginning. How could I convey that this really wasn't about me?

Conversations with my pastor helped me realize that sharing my story would be testifying to God's goodness, not my own. When my intended recipient and I shared the story with our congregation, it was God who received that standing ovation. It was God who was thanked and praised.

In this Holy Week, we remember what Christ accomplished for the world. But his work did not end on the cross, nor did it end at the empty tomb. Christ is alive, and we are his body; he continues to accomplish all things through us. Sometimes we're powerfully aware of God at work in us; other times we think nothing of the difference God is making through actions we might deem ordinary or small.

Did you pray for someone today? Did you show up at an AA meeting? Did you say thank you to a cashier? God is blessing the world through you. Share your stories; God will be working through your witness too.

Prayer

God, you are bold in your fierce love for us. Help us to be bold in proclaiming your goodness, acknowledging that you are blessing the world through us. To you be given thanks and praise! Amen.

April 1

Romans 8:31-32

If God is for us, who is against us? He who did not withhold his own Son but gave him up for all of us, how will he not with him also give us everything else?

To ponder

Unexpected and mysterious is the gentle word of grace.
Ever loving and sustaining is the peace of God's embrace.
If we falter in our courage and we doubt what we have known,
God is faithful to console us as a mother tends her own.
—"Unexpected and mysterious," ELW 258

Room for you

The night before we dropped off our oldest son at college, I had a dream in which the campus looked nothing like it had when we visited. Everything was run down; buildings looked as though they might collapse at any time. Crumbled parking lots were surrounded by barbed wire.

It was a relief the next morning when the campus was just as beautiful as I remembered it, complete with returning students calling out words of welcome. I still cried when we drove away, but I knew we were leaving our child in a good place.

I can't wrap my head around God freely giving Jesus to a world determined to destroy him. From the moment of his birth, Jesus threatened the powerful. King Herod wanted the newborn baby Jesus dead, and he slaughtered countless innocent children in an attempt to secure his own power. Coming to dwell with us, Jesus was immediately put at terrible risk. How could God stand to let go?

I imagine the heart of God broke wide open in sending Jesus to enter fully into our human experience, just as the heavens were torn apart when Jesus was baptized by John. In the embrace of a brokenhearted God, there becomes room not just for the beloved Son but for all of God's beloved children. There is room for you.

Prayer

Mothering God, you have given us everything. Today we thank you for holding all creation to your heart. Amen.

April 2 / Maundy Thursday

Romans 8:33-34

Who will bring any charge against God's elect? It is God who justifies. Who is to condemn? It is Christ who died, or rather, who was raised, who is also at the right hand of God, who also intercedes for us.

To ponder

I define shame as the intensely painful feeling or experience of believing that we are flawed and therefore unworthy of love and belonging—something we've experienced, done, or failed to do makes us unworthy of connection.—Brené Brown, "Shame vs. Guilt"

No place for shame

Guilt might serve you well for a time, leading you to apologize and to change your ways. Shame, though, is never helpful. Shame makes you question not what you've done but who you actually are. Tonight's liturgy includes an invitation to come forward and kneel for the laying on of hands. The guilt you bear with you to the altar is removed at the command of Jesus, and you need never pick it up again. You are forgiven. Can you leave your shame at the altar too?

So often, the one who tries to condemn me is me. But not tonight. Tonight I'm at the table with Jesus as he kneels to wash the feet of his disciples, even the one who will soon deny him three times. Tonight I'm at the table with Judas as Jesus shares the bread—his very body—with even the one who has conspired to have him arrested. Tonight Jesus gathers me, and you, and all creation, and holds us together with love.

We, the condemned and the condemning, are released tonight from guilt and shame. We can breathe deeply. We can stretch our hands to the sky in praise. We can leave the table and go into the world with the confidence that we are worthy of love, because God has made it so.

Prayer

God of love, you create us in your image and refuse to condemn us. Free us from guilt and shame, so that, unburdened, we might love one another—and ourselves—as you so love us. Amen.

April 3 / Good Friday

Romans 8:35, 37

Who will separate us from the love of Christ? Will affliction or distress or persecution or famine or nakedness or peril or sword? . . . No, in all these things we are more than victorious through him who loved us.

To ponder

It's not that I'm unaware of the suffering and the soon-to-be suffering in the world; it's that I know the suffering exists beside wet grass and a bright blue sky recently scrubbed by rain. The beauty and the suffering are equally true.—Ann Patchett, *Tom Lake*

Love's victory

Suffering is true. It's as solid as the cross upon which we gaze this day. It tries to persuade us to give up on making a difference, hit snooze on the alarms of our empathy, and pull the covers over our heads. But beauty is also true, even on this day when we are asked to stop turning away and instead look directly at the worst the forces of evil can do.

The cross is death, but it is also abundant life. It is the experience of God-forsakenness, but it is also the promise that we are never alone. The cross of Christ is an end, but it is also a brave beginning. It is defeat, but it is also, and even more so, love's ultimate victory.

The canyons of despair are deep, but the love of God refuses to abandon us there. On the very cross that was intended to be an instrument of death, Christ raises us to life and illumines for us the beauty that is ours to proclaim to a weary world—transforming forgiveness, grace as vast as the bluest sky, love that never dies.

Prayer

Beautiful Savior, it is easy to become overwhelmed by suffering. Draw near to us as we sit with the grief of this day, point us to the beauty of your victorious love, and help us cling fiercely to your promise of redeeming love for all the world. Amen.

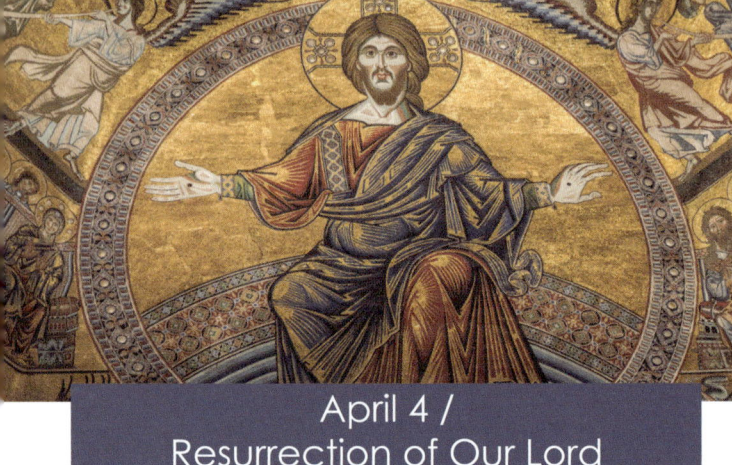

April 4 / Resurrection of Our Lord

Romans 8:38-39

For I am convinced that neither death, nor life, nor angels, nor rulers, nor things present, nor things to come, nor powers, nor height, nor depth, nor anything else in all creation will be able to separate us from the love of God in Christ Jesus our Lord.

To ponder

The primary task of the Church . . . is to celebrate with joy the salvific action of the Lord in history.—Gustavo Gutiérrez, *A Theology of Liberation*

This is the night

Joy. Sometimes it comes in electric, extraordinary ways—a baby born, a life transformed, a stone rolled away to reveal an empty tomb. Sometimes it comes in gentle, daily bread—a song, a meal, a word, a walk. Always, it is the Holy Spirit's gift to you, given in baptism and renewed each day.

As we journey through Lent and through life, we increasingly understand that we are people in need of a savior. We cannot free ourselves from all that robs us of life; we are powerless in the face of sin and death. God understands our need and sends Jesus to shepherd us through death to life abundant.

"This is the night," we proclaim in the Easter Vigil, "in which, breaking the chains of death, Christ arises from hell in triumph!" Jesus, our risen Savior, ensures this night that nothing will ever separate us from the love of God. This is the truth that empowers us to live as followers of Jesus, trusting God to lead us into a future filled with hope, sharing with all those we encounter the joy of being known and saved by the love of God outpoured for all this weary world.

This is the night! Christ is risen! Alleluia!

Prayer

God of life abundant, we celebrate with joy your steadfast love poured out for us through the life, death, and resurrection of Jesus, our Savior. Empower us to live with the confidence that we are never alone but are always supported, sustained, and saved by your love. Amen.

Notes

February 18: Marva J. Dawn, *In the Beginning, God* (InterVarsity, 2009), 17. **February 19:** Mother Teresa of Calcutta, *In My Own Words*, ed. José Luis González-Balado (Gramercy, 1996), 5. **February 20:** Nelson Mandela, preface to *Mandela's Way* by Richard Stengel (Broadway, 2018), xi. **February 21:** Ernst Käsemann, "The Righteousness of God in Paul," in *New Testament Questions of Today*, trans. W. J. Montague (Fortress, 1969), 180, 182. **February 22:** Martin Luther, "Preface to the Epistle of St. Paul to the Romans," *Luther's Works*, ed. Jaroslav Pelikan and Helmut T. Lehmann (Fortress, 1960), 35:370. **February 23:** Nadia Bolz-Weber, *Pastrix* (Worthy, 2021), xix–xx. **February 24:** Luther, "Preface to the Epistle of St. Paul to the Romans," 370. Prayer: See Mark 9:24. **February 25:** Paulo Coelho de Souza, @paulocoelho, Twitter, June 2, 2012. **February 26:** Malala Yousafzai, *I Am Malala* (Weidenfeld & Nicolson, 2014). **February 27:** Thich Nhat Hanh, *True Love* (Shambhala, 2006), 4. **February 28:** Rachel Held Evans, *Searching for Sunday* (Thomas Nelson, 2015), 73. **March 1:** Tikhon Mollard, "Homily for Sunday, August 8, 2021," Orthodox Church in America, www.oca.org/reflections/metropolitan-tikhon/homily-for-sunday-august-8-2021. **March 2:** Munther Isaac, *The Other Side of the Wall* (IVP, 2020). **March 3:** Richard Rohr, *Falling Upward* (Jossey-Bass, 2023). **March 5:** African American spiritual, "Oh, Freedom," public domain. **March 6:** Martin Luther, *Commentary on Romans*, trans. J. Theodore Mueller (Concordia, 1954). **March 7:** A. A. Milne, *Winnie-the-Pooh* (Methuen, 1926). **March 8:** Henri J. M. Nouwen, *The Way of the Heart* (HarperOne, 1997). **March 9:** Cheryl M. Peterson, *The Holy Spirit in the Christian Life* (Baker Academic, 2024), 45. **March 10:** Isaac, *Other Side of the Wall*, 177. **March 11:** Robin Wall Kimmerer, *Braiding Sweetgrass* (Milkweed Editions, 2015), 308. **March 12:** Resmaa Menakem, *My Grandmother's Hands* (Central Recovery Press, 2017), 25. **March 13:** Susan Briehl and Tom Witt, *Holden Prayer Around the Cross* (Augsburg Fortress, 2009), 93–94. **March 14:** Joe Davis, *Unearthing Us* (Sparkhouse, 2024), 71. **March 15:** Thich Nhat Hanh, *Living Buddha, Living Christ* (Riverhead, 1995), 9. **March 16:** Mark S. Hanson, former ELCA presiding bishop, at the installation of Kirby Unti as bishop of the ELCA's Northwest Washington Synod, September 15, 2013. **March 17:** St. Patrick, public domain. **March 18:** Text: Thomas á Kempis, 1380–1471; trans. Benjamin Webb, 1819–1885, alt.; "O love, how deep," ELW 322, st. 1. **March 19:** Kate Morton, *The Forgotten Garden* (Simon & Schuster, 2009), 408. **March 20:** Evans, *Searching for Sunday*, xvi. **March 21:** Max De Pree, *Leadership Is an Art* (Currency, 2004), excerpted from https://leadershipnow.com/Max_DePree_What_Is_Leadership.html. **March 22:** Kathleen Norris, *The Quotidian Mysteries* (Paulist, 1998), 70. **March 23:** Priya Parker, *The Art of Gathering* (Penguin, 2018), 229. **March 24:** M. Scott Peck, *People of the Lie* (Touchstone 1983), 181. **March 25:** Jenny Lawson, *Furiously Happy* (Flatiron, 2015), 249. **March 26:** Atul Gawande, *Being Mortal* (Henry Holt, 2014), 232. **March 27:** Michael B. Curry, *Love Is the Way* (Penguin, 2020), 218–19. **March 28:** Henri J. M. Nouwen, *Home Tonight* (Random House, 2009). **March 29:** Neichelle R. Guidry, *Curating a World* (MMGI Books, 2016), 75. **March 30:** Sarah Bessey, "It's No Small Thing," *Sarah Bessey's Field Notes* (Substack), November 19, 2024, https://sarahbessey.substack.com/p/no-small-thing. **March 31:** John O'Donohue, *To Bless the Space Between Us* (Convergent, 2008), 207. **April 1:** Text © 2002 Jeanette M. Lindholm, b. 1961, admin. Augsburg Fortress; "Unexpected and mysterious," ELW 258, st.1. **April 2:** Brené Brown, "Shame vs. Guilt," January 15, 2013, https://brenebrown.com/articles/2013/01/15/shame-v-guilt/. **April 3:** Ann Patchett, *Tom Lake* (HarperCollins, 2023), 253. **April 4:** Gustavo Gutiérrez, *A Theology of Liberation* (Orbis Books, 1988), 150.